MANIPULATION
Cutting the Strings of Control

JUNE HUNT

ROSE PUBLISHING/ASPIRE PRESS

Torrance, California

ROSE PUBLISHING/ASPIRE PRESS

Manipulation: Cutting the Strings of Control
Copyright © 2013 Hope For The Heart
All rights reserved.
Aspire Press, a division of Rose Publishing, Inc.
4733 Torrance Blvd., #259
Torrance, California 90503 USA
www.aspirepress.com

Register your book at www.aspirepress.com/register
Get inspiration via email, sign up at www.aspirepress.com

Printed by Regent Publishing Services Ltd.
Printed in China
February 2015, 3rd printing

CONTENTS

Dear friend,

When I was in grade school, all the students were asked to sell raffle tickets door-to-door in order to raise money for our school. Now, *that* was the point—to raise money *for the school*. However, I didn't think that cause sounded nearly as compelling as it could be.

So I went door-to-door telling homeowners how they could be the *lucky winner* of a brand new color television set (which was true)—but then I gave a "bleeding heart" story of where this money was going: "*to help poor, sick children in the hospital*"—which was in no way true!

By the way, the boy and girl who sold the most tickets would be awarded a prize—a watch! I wanted to win that pink, plastic watch so much I could taste it! Well, I hate to admit it—but I won. (In truth, I won only because my brother, a year older, gave me some of his tickets—he was far ahead of all the other students.)

Ultimately, I won the girl's watch by dishonest, manipulative means, whereas Ray won the boy's watch by honest, persuasive means.

Why didn't I tell the truth? Because I was determined to win that pink watch, I thought I needed to control the outcome. And that's precisely the point of manipulation: *control*.

Now consider this: Apart from the obvious deception, what is the deeper problem with manipulation? Choosing to manipulate people is the opposite of choosing to trust God—trusting Him with everything in our lives.

What a change I experienced when I finally gave Christ control of my life! The comforting promise of Proverbs 3:5–6 became my inspiration: *"Trust in the LORD with all your heart, And lean not on your own understanding; In all your ways acknowledge Him, And He shall direct your paths."* (NKJV)

Even though I had experienced a true change through Christ in most areas of my life, periodically I kept finding myself in an insidious pit, and I didn't know how to climb out of it. Oddly enough, rather than growing up as the "master manipulator," I kept letting others manipulate me. At times I knew I was "caving in" to manipulation—however, I honestly thought I had no choice. However, I *did* have a choice. Nevertheless, I lived as a "peace-at-any-price" person: afraid of the anger of others, afraid to set a "boundary," and afraid of disapproval.

At times I would violate my own conscience: I would say *yes* to people when I wanted to say *no*. Again, I thought I had no choice.

Does this situation sound too familiar? Do you say *yes* to people when you know you should say *no*? Do you even know when you're being manipulated, yet feel powerless to stop it? If so, I understand!

A major turning point in my life came when I was confronted face-to-face with the Word of

God—one single verse that challenged me to say *no* to manipulative people: *"Am I now trying to win the approval of men, or of God? Or am I trying to please men? If I were still trying to please men, I would not be a servant of Christ"* (Galatians 1:10).

What a revelation! What relief! What reassurance! I finally realized that I had the right to say *no* to people so I could say *yes* to God!

And that is true for you. Realize that manipulation is the number one guilt game. This means manipulative people will try to make you feel guilty of insensitivity, of disloyalty, of whatever, in order to pressure you into giving your time, your money, yourself even though you are not being led by the Lord to do so.

This book on manipulation is produced so that you will learn what tactics are used in manipulation, why you have been manipulated, and how to stop being manipulated; in other words, to enable you to say *no* to people so you can say *yes* to God.

Don't forget—Jesus said, *"If the Son sets you free, you will be free indeed"* (John 8:36). My prayer is that through the truths within these pages, you will find hope for your heart to live in His freedom.

Yours in the Lord's hope,

June Hunt

MANIPULATION
Cutting the Strings of Control

It is handed down from one generation to the next ... to the next ... and to the next. But this family trait has no genetic history of big ears or blue eyes—no DNA of fair skin or brown freckles. This is something behavioral, something willful, something bad, called *manipulation*.

This behavior—found in men and women alike—can also be called a character flaw. In fact, this pattern of conniving and cover-up periodically appears throughout the entire human family, even in the least likely family line: the patriarchs of the Bible—Abraham, Isaac, and Jacob, as well as in Jacob's sons and their descendants. Each of these men, and their wives, manipulated people and circumstances in an attempt to dictate their own destinies or to circumvent some assumed negative consequences.

It's clear—sometimes the faith of the patriarchs faltered and gave way to fear. And too many times the results were grave: dishonor to their name and disgrace to their God. And all because of maniacal *manipulation*!

Truly ...

> "There is a way that seems right to a man,
> but in the end it leads to death."
> (Proverbs 14:12)

DEFINITIONS

Abraham's wife, Sarah, has long been considered to be submissive—however, she can also be seen as subversive.

In the Bible, she is praised as a woman of inner beauty, *"who obeyed Abraham and called him her master"* (1 Peter 3:6). But she tarnished that inner beauty by manipulating circumstances to force God's promise to Abraham to be fulfilled—in her timing. God had assured Abraham that his descendants would be as numerous as the sands of the sea. But now the couple is aged; they are still barren. Since Sarah is now well past childbearing years, she proposes a plan to be sure God's promise is on her calendar!

"Go, sleep with my maidservant; perhaps I can build a family through her" (Genesis 16:2).

Abraham agrees and sleeps with Hagar, who, in turn, births a son named Ishmael, a son through whom the covenant promises were never intended and would never be fulfilled.

Abraham and Sarah have not yet learned that …

"The plans of the Lord stand firm forever,
the purposes of his heart
through all generations."
(Psalm 33:11)

She is 65 years old—and *stunning*.

Since the life span of the patriarchs was twice that of people today, Sarai is doubtless in her prime, and that poses a serious threat to her husband, Abram (later called Sarah and Abraham, respectively).

The couple sets off for Egypt to escape a famine, but before setting foot into the foreign land, Abram decides to "fabricate" a tale, twisting the truth. This first patriarch of the faith fears for his life because if the Egyptians discover he is married to beautiful Sarai, they might kill him in order to take her into Pharaoh's harem.

So he twists the truth: *"I know what a beautiful woman you are. ... Say you are my sister, so that I will be treated well for your sake and my life will be spared because of you"* (Genesis 12:11–13).

Bottom line: Abram manipulates the facts. Indeed, she is his half sister, but also fully his wife. Thus, rather than trusting God, the cycle of manipulation begins.

▶ **Manipulation** is the art of controlling people or circumstances by indirect, unfair, or deceptive means—especially to one's own advantage.[1]

▶ **Manipulation** happens to those who allow others to have excessive control over them— the control that God alone should have.

The Bible is clear about not giving others too much control, too much power, and too much authority. We must not allow another person to take the place only God should have. Instead we should apply the first of the Ten Commandments:

"You shall have no other gods before me." (Exodus 20:3)

WHAT IS Persuasion?

Although Sarai is indeed Abram's half sister, this plan is all about a cover-up, and Sarai complies.

Once in Egypt, Sarai catches the eye of more than one court official, and soon she is whisked away to Pharaoh's palace. Abram, of course, gets the royal treatment as well, *"for her sake,"* acquiring *"sheep and cattle, male and female donkeys, menservants and maidservants, and camels"* (Genesis 12:16).

But while Abram is pampered, Pharaoh is pummeled. God inflicts grave diseases on Pharaoh and his household because he has taken Abram's wife, not merely his half sister.

Sternly, Pharaoh confronts Abram. *"'What have you done to me?' he said. 'Why didn't you tell me she was your wife? Why did you say, "She is my sister," so that I took her to be my wife? Now then, here is your wife. Take her and go!'"* (Genesis 12:18–19).

How much better it would have been had Abram stuck with the truth, trusted God, and appealed to

Pharaoh's mind rather than trying to manipulate his emotions.

> "I have chosen the way of truth;
> I have set my heart on your laws."
> (Psalm 119:30)

▶ **Persuasion** is the act of convincing others by urging, reasoning, and appealing to their minds.[2]

▶ **Persuasion** is the process of winning over others by logical arguments and sound reasoning.

No other missionary for Christ is more well-known or more well-thought-of than the apostle Paul. He set the standard for how the gospel of Christ is to be shared with all people everywhere. And it is not through manipulation, but through persuasion.

> "Every Sabbath he reasoned in the synagogue, trying to persuade Jews and Greeks. ... 'This man,' they charged, 'is persuading the people to worship God in ways contrary to the law.'"
> (Acts 18:4, 13)

Manipulation or Persuasion

QUESTION: "What is the difference between manipulation and persuasion?"

ANSWER:

▶ Those who manipulate use dishonest emotions to achieve their goal.

▶ Those who persuade use honest reason to achieve their goal.

The Bible speaks plainly about our need to appeal to others by using accurate reasoning.

> "Unlike so many ... In Christ we speak before God with sincerity, like men sent from God. ... We have renounced secret and shameful ways; we do not use deception ... By setting forth the truth plainly we commend ourselves to every man's conscience in the sight of God."
> **(2 Corinthians 2:17; 4:2)**

Now Sarah is 90 years old—and apparently still a knockout.

This time the king of Gerar will be the recipient of the couple's conniving. After Abraham again identifies Sarah as "his sister"—out of fear for his own life—King Abimelech takes Sarah for his harem.

God intervenes this time not with serious diseases as with Pharaoh, but with the most stern, most horrifying warning: *"You are as good as dead because of the woman you have taken; she is a married woman"* (Genesis 20:3).

Abimelech—perplexed, petrified, and perturbed —pleads his case before God, *"LORD, will you destroy an innocent nation? Did he not say to me, 'She is my sister,' and didn't she also say, 'He is my brother'? I have done this with a clear conscience and clean hands"* (Genesis 20:4–5).

In a dream the Lord acknowledges the king's innocence, and unveils His sovereign protection that had kept Abimelech from touching Sarah. Then the Lord gives this instruction: *"Now return the man's wife, for he is a prophet, and he will pray for you and you will live. But if you do not return her, you may be sure that you and all yours will die"* (Genesis 20:7).

Some lessons are hard to learn! It's been 25 years since Sarah and Abraham's first lesson, but trusting God doesn't always come easily. Manipulation, on the other hand, seems to come easily, even for the people of God, especially when it looks effective on the surface.

Clearly, although spiritual abuse is a relatively new term, it has been occurring for a very long time. Spiritual manipulation involves:

▶ The use of **religious words or acts** to manipulate someone for personal gain or to achieve a personal agenda, thereby harming that person's walk with God.

▶ At the core of spiritual manipulation is control of others. Spiritual manipulation is acting "spiritual" to benefit oneself by using self-centered efforts to control others.

> **A**cting "spiritual" to
>
> **B**enefit oneself by
>
> **U**sing
>
> **S**elf-centered
>
> **E**fforts to control others

Spiritual manipulation was a problem even in the earliest days of the Christian church.

> **"There are many rebellious people, mere talkers and deceivers. ...**
> **They are ruining whole households by teaching things they ought not to teach."**
> **(Titus 1:10–11)**

EXAMPLES:

▶ **The religious leader** who uses guilt to compel attendance, financial giving, or service

▶ **The religious counselor** who takes emotional or sexual advantage of a counselee in the name of "comfort or compassion"

▶ **The religious people** who accuse those who disagree with them of being rebellious against God

▶ **The religious husband** who demands submission from his wife as a means of control, getting her to placate his selfishness

▶ **The religious parent** who commands total, unquestioned compliance from children and uses harsh discipline, without compassion or understanding

▶ **The religious employer** who micromanages employees, expecting them to work long hours without equitable monetary compensation

Spiritual manipulators put confidence in their "position of authority" and their perceived right to use those under their influence to accomplish their own personal agenda. However, God alone has the wisdom, the power, and the right to accomplish His plans and purposes for those whom He has created.

> "In his heart a man plans his course,
> but the Lord determines his steps."
> (Proverbs 16:9)

King Abimelech returns Sarah, but not before confronting Abraham "one-on-one" about his manipulative deception. *"How have I wronged you that you have brought such great guilt upon me and my kingdom? You have done things to me that should not be done. ... What was your reason for doing this?"* (Genesis 20:9–10).

Abraham fumbles with feeble excuses: *"I said to myself, 'There is surely no fear of God in this place, and they will kill me because of my wife.' Besides, she really is my sister ... I said to her, 'This is how you can show your love to me: Everywhere we go, say of me, 'He is my brother' "* (Genesis 20:11–13).

Abimelech extends gracious gifts to the reunited couple, and Abraham prays on behalf of the king, for *"The LORD had closed up every womb in Abimelech's household because of Abraham's wife Sarah"* (Genesis 20:18). There are indeed negative consequences to our deceptive manipulation. Sadly, wrong assumptions can lead to wrong actions, and manipulation of relationships is often the result.

▶ **To manipulate** is to unduly restrain, restrict, or rule in a relationship by use of deception.

▶ **To manipulate** is to suppress or oppress a person by subversive overt or covert tactics.

▶ **To manipulate** is to have excessive, cunning control.

However, God alone is to rule and reign over us.

The Bible warns …

"You shall have no other gods before me."
(Deuteronomy 5:7)

WHAT DOES It Mean to Be Manipulated?

The town of Gerar is beset with guile—*again*.

This time Abraham's son Isaac and his beautiful wife, Rebekah, will do the duping, and poor King Abimelech will become a victim of manipulation.

Isaac fears that the men of Gerar might kill him if he reveals that Rebekah is his wife, so he takes a page from his dad's book: *"She is my sister"* (Genesis 20:2; 26:7). The same deceptive words are uttered by father and son on two separate occasions—simply to shield the truth, simply because of fear.

The couple carries off the cover-up for a significant period of time until King Abimelech "happens" to cast a downward glance through a window and sees Isaac and Rebekah, not having a sibling squabble—but *caressing*.

The king summons Isaac and fires off accusations and questions. *"She is really your wife! Why did you say, 'She is my sister'? … What is this you have done to us? One of the men might well have slept with your wife, and you would have brought guilt upon us"* (Genesis 26:9–10).

Like Abraham, Isaac expresses his fear for his life, and Abimelech gives orders throughout the land that anyone who harms Isaac and Rebekah will be killed. *And also like Abraham, Isaac, the second patriarch of the faith, succumbs to fear ... and resorts to manipulation.*

Once more faith is forgotten. Once more someone is manipulated. Once more someone is misled. Once more someone suffers.

To be manipulated is to allow:

▶ Another person to dictate your thoughts, feelings, and behaviors

▶ Decisions to be made for you

▶ Others to have control over you, rather than allowing God to control you

Scripture tells us ...

> **"The mind controlled by the Spirit is life and peace."**
> **(Romans 8:6)**

The fabric of fear and the mantle of manipulation have passed from Abraham to Isaac and from Sarah to Rebekah, from father to son and from mother-in-law to daughter-in-law. And it does not stop there. This sin mushrooms into the third and fourth generations, and beyond, to an even greater generational maze. Like all other sins, manipulation continues until it comes face-to-face with faith—the antithesis of fear.

> "He [Jesus] said to his disciples, 'Why are you so afraid? Do you still have no faith?'"
> (Mark 4:40)

The Patriarchs, Their Wives, and Their Families

▶ **Abram and Sarai manipulate Pharaoh** into thinking they are not husband and wife (Genesis 12:11–13, 17–19).

▶ **Barren Sarai manipulates circumstances** to build a family for herself through her maidservant Hagar (Genesis 16:1–2).

▶ **Aged Sarah attempts to manipulate the Lord** by denying she had laughed when He said she would give birth to a son (Genesis 18:10–15).

▶ **Abraham and Sarah manipulate King Abimelech** into thinking they are not husband and wife (Genesis 20:2, 4–5).

- **Jacob manipulates his brother Esau** by bartering his birthright for a meal of lentil stew (Genesis 25:29–34).

- **Isaac and Rebekah manipulate King Abimelech** (of Gerar) into thinking they are not husband and wife (Genesis 26:7, 9–10).

- **Rebekah and Jacob manipulate Esau and Isaac** to secure birthright blessings for Jacob (Genesis chapter 27).

- **Rebekah manipulates Isaac** persuading him to agree to send Jacob to her brother Laban by claiming she feared he might otherwise marry a Hittite woman (Genesis 27:46).

- **Uncle Laban manipulates Jacob** on his wedding night by giving him—not Rachel—but her older sister Leah (Genesis 29:21–25).

- **Barren Rachel manipulates Jacob** to build a family for herself through her maidservant Bilhah (Genesis 30:1–3).

- **Leah, unable to continue bearing children, manipulates Jacob** to continue building her family through her maidservant Zilpah (Genesis 30:9–12).

- **Rachel manipulates Leah** into giving her some of her son's mandrakes, an aphrodisiac she hoped might help her become pregnant, in exchange for a night with Jacob (Genesis 30:14–16).

- ▶ **Laban manipulates Jacob's ability** to acquire a large herd from among his livestock as they agree to go their separate ways (Genesis 30:31–43).

- ▶ **Rachel manipulates Laban** by stealing his household gods and sitting on them inside her camel's saddle while he searches her tent in vain (Genesis 31:19, 34–35).

- ▶ **Jacob manipulates Laban** by secretly leaving for Gilead with his family and all of his possessions (Genesis 31:20, 26–29).

- ▶ **Jacob's sons manipulate the Canaanites** to be circumcised so that while they are still weak in recovery, the brothers can massacre the rapists who violated their sister (Genesis 34:13–17, 24–29).

CHARACTERISTIC METHODS OF MANIPULATORS

His name says it all.

After nine months of jostling in Rebekah's womb, Jacob comes into the world just behind Esau, his hand grasping Esau's heel. The name *Jacob* means "heel catcher," but its significance also stretches further into time when Jacob's character will one day mirror the name's additional meanings— "trickster" and "supplanter."[3]

The two brothers couldn't be more different. *Esau* is extroverted and brash and a skillful hunter; *Jacob* is introverted and quiet, a cook who prefers spending his days at home. *Esau* is described as "hairy"; *Jacob* is described as "smooth." *Esau* has the favor of his father, Isaac; *Jacob* has the favor of his mother, Rebekah.

Jacob's manipulative ways will manifest themselves in adulthood when another jostling of sorts occurs over Esau's birthright.

Esau would later say of Jacob …

> **"Isn't he rightly named Jacob?**
> **He has deceived me these two times."**
> **(Genesis 27:36)**

"Quick, let me have some of that red stew! I'm famished!" (Genesis 25:30).

Esau has just returned from the countryside with one thing on his mind—his stomach. Once he gets a whiff of the thick, red, lentil stew Jacob is cooking, he is willing to satisfy his hunger pangs at all costs.

Esau does indeed get a delicious bowl of stew along with some bread and something to drink, but it costs him dearly! Jacob offers the stew on one condition: Esau must give him his birthright.

As their father Isaac is now aged and approaching death, the loss of the birthright blessing will soon leave Esau with a very bad taste in his mouth.

And so it generally goes with those who partake of the foul game of manipulation. Yet those who play the game of manipulation have an entirely different perspective, as do Jacob and his mother, Rebekah.

▶ **Manipulative Power Players**[4]

- Use verbal and physical abuse to gain power
- Use put-downs to get position
- Dominate conversations to get control
- Use threats to intimidate
- Say anything to humiliate

Goal: To manipulate by implying, "I am right and you are wrong."

"They make their tongues as sharp as a serpent's; the poison of vipers is on their lips." (Psalm 140:3)

▶ **Manipulative Martyrs**[5]

- Scold others to make them feel sad
- Blame others to make them feel bad
- Play the "guilt game" to make others feel at fault
- Shame others to make them feel sorry
- Play the victim to make others feel pity

Goal: To manipulate by implying: "It's all your fault. How could you treat me this way?"

"The tongue that brings healing is a tree of life, but a deceitful tongue crushes the spirit." (Proverbs 15:4)

▶ **Manipulative Rescuers**

- Provide unsolicited help to make others feel obligated
- Assist others—even when not wanted—to gain a sense of indebtedness
- Help others to make them feel ingratiated
- Give exaggerated care to cause others to feel commitment
- Extend aid in order to coerce others

Goal: To manipulate by implying: "After all I have done for you, now you owe me."

"All a man's ways seem right to him, but the LORD weighs the heart." (Proverbs 21:2)

▶ **Manipulative People Pleasers**[6]

- Use charm to gain the favor of others
- Praise others to gain approval
- Accommodate others to gain appreciation
- Extend favors to gain gratitude
- Do kind acts to gain loyalty

Goal: To manipulate by implying: "After all I've done to please you, you should please me."

"Charm is deceptive." (Proverbs 31:30)

WHAT ARE the Eight **S**'s of Verbal Manipulation?

Like mother, like son.

The time has come and Isaac is ready to bestow the birthright blessing upon his oldest son, Esau—apparently oblivious to the bartering between Jacob and Esau for a mere bowl of stew. Rebekah overhears Isaac telling Esau to go hunt some wild game and prepare him some *"tasty food,"* and then he will give his firstborn his blessing (Genesis 27:4).

Immediately Rebekah's manipulative mind begins strategizing, taking full advantage of one critical factor concerning her husband: He can no longer see.

No sooner has Esau walked out the door when Rebekah gives the following instructions to

Jacob: *"Now, my son, listen carefully and do what I tell you: Go out to the flock and bring me two choice young goats, so I can prepare some tasty food for your father, just the way he likes it. Then take it to your father to eat, so that he may give you his blessing before he dies"* (Genesis 27:8–10).

Jacob's mind reels with questions: *"But my brother Esau is a hairy man, and I'm a man with smooth skin. What if my father touches me?"* (Genesis 27:11–12).

Jacob fears becoming the recipient of a curse rather than a blessing, but Rebekah accepts full responsibility and proceeds with her plot. And as it turns out, the goats will be useful for more than just "tasty food."

And the scheming and conniving go on, with one verbal game after another.

Verbal Methods of Playing the Game[7]

1 The Subversive Schemer

- Scheming to plot a deceptive plan
- Scheming to distort reality
- Scheming by telling half-truths
- Scheming by misrepresentation

▶ **The Bible addresses how God deals with schemers.**

"He [God] catches the wise in their craftiness, and the schemes of the wily are swept away." (Job 5:13)

▶ **The manipulator implies ...**

"If you don't willingly do what I want, I will trick you into doing it."

2 Scheming Should's[8]

- "You should show me respect."
- "You should meet my needs."
- "You should make me happy."
- "You should give me security."

▶ **In contrast, the Bible says ...**

"[Love] is not self-seeking" (1 Corinthians 13:5)

▶ **The manipulator implies ...**

"If you don't meet my expectations, you are guilty of neglect."

3 Strident Screaming[9]

- Yelling to apply pressure
- Yelling to unnerve
- Yelling to publicly humiliate
- Yelling to intimidate

▶ **Psalm 64:3–4 says ...**

"They sharpen their tongues like swords and aim their words like deadly arrows."

▶ **The manipulator implies ...**

"If you don't do what I want, I'll make you wish you had."

4 Sarcastic Swords[10]

- Stabbing with cutting humor
- Stabbing with jabbing words
- Stabbing with put-downs
- Stabbing with malicious mocking

▶ **The Bible says those who crucified Jesus ...**

"Twisted together a crown of thorns and set it on his head. They put a staff in his right hand and knelt in front of him and mocked him. 'Hail, king of the Jews!'" (Matthew 27:29)

▶ **The manipulator implies ...**

"If you aren't what I want you to be, I will use words to wound you."

5 Sexual Seduction[11]

- Seductive talk
- Suggestive clothing
- Sensual advertising
- Sexual body movements

▶ **The book of Proverbs warns about the manipulative, seductive woman ...**

"With persuasive words she led him astray; she seduced him with her smooth talk. All at once he followed her like an ox going to the slaughter, like a deer stepping into a noose" (Proverbs 7:21–22).

▶ **The manipulator implies ...**

"If you don't buy what I'm selling, you are not going to be macho."

6 Showering Sentiments[12]

- Excessive praise to appeal to the ego

- Excessive gifts to create a sense of obligation

- Excessive affection to gain a sexual or emotional advantage

- Excessive money to buy control

▶ **In contrast, Proverbs 26:28 says ...**

"A flattering mouth works ruin."

▶ **The manipulator implies ...**

"If you don't respond to my generosity by doing what I want you to do, you are ungrateful."

7 Sly Suggestions[13]

- *Guilt Game #1*: A wife says, "John just bought Sara a new car. It must be nice to be so loved."

- *Guilt Game #2*: A husband says, "Mary encourages her husband to go out with the guys any time he wants, for as long as he wants. He's lucky to have such a wife."

- *Guilt Game #3*: A "friend" says to another friend, "Chris has a friend who will give him any amount of money—no questions asked. Now that is a true friend."

- **Guilt Game #4**: A teenager says to parents, "None of my friends have a curfew. It must be nice to have such trusting parents."

▶ **Proverbs 26:24 describes the manipulator ...**

"A malicious man disguises himself with his lips, but in his heart he harbors deceit."

▶ **The manipulator implies ...**

"You ought to meet my every need, and if you don't, I'll make you feel guilty."

8 Sympathy Seekers[14]

- Speaking and acting needy intentionally
- Speaking and acting pitiful with "pity parties"
- Speaking and acting helpless and childlike
- Speaking and acting hopeless unless a rescuer arrives

Instead of expecting others to carry your load when you could carry it yourself ...

▶ **The Bible says ...**

"Each one should carry his own load" (Galatians 6:5).

▶ **The manipulator implies ...**

"You should take care of my heart, and if you don't, you are callous and cruel."

Rebekah covers Jacob's hands and neck in goat hair and puts Esau's best clothes on him. The ruse is now complete. Jacob is the personification of Esau, down to the smell of the outdoors that wafts through Esau's clothing.

"Esau" presents himself before Isaac, who may be blind today—but who wasn't born yesterday! Isaac inquires about the short time span it took "Esau" to find and cook the game, and instantly recognizes Jacob's voice but is perplexed by his "hairy hands."

As Jacob responds to his father's inquiries, the portrait of deceit becomes colored with more than just manipulation. The quickly served meal? *"The LORD your God gave me success"* (Genesis 27: 20), Jacob lies. Are you really Esau? *"I am"* (Genesis 27:24), Jacob lies again.

And the birthright blessing ensues. *"May God give you of heaven's dew and of earth's richness— an abundance of grain and new wine. May nations serve you and peoples bow down to you. Be lord over your brothers, and may the sons of your mother bow down to you. May those who curse you be cursed and those who bless you be blessed"* (Genesis 27: 28–29).

Thus, this manipulative maze incorporates deceptive words and actions with blatant lies and "hairy hands."

Non-Verbal Methods of Playing the Manipulation Game[15]

1 Situation Seizer

- Uses the poor judgment of others to receive personal promotion
- Uses the poor health of others to receive personal profit
- Uses the problems of others to receive personal praise
- Uses the pain of others to receive personal progress

▶ **In contrast, Scripture admonishes …**

"Do nothing out of selfish ambition or vain conceit, but in humility consider others better than yourselves" (Philippians 2:3).

▶ **The manipulator implies …**

"My wants and wishes supersede those of everyone else."

2 Silent Treatment[16]

- Pouting, brooding, and ignoring
- Coldly turning away from your spouse
- Not answering the phone, emails, or texts as punishment
- Refusing to speak to an offender

▶ **Scripture says …**

"When I was silent and still, not even saying anything good, my anguish increased" (Psalm 39:2).

▶ **The manipulator implies ...**

"If you don't do what I want, you don't get my approval, my communication—or me."

3 Slam/Bam Slamming

- Slamming drawers
- Slamming doors
- Slamming phones
- Slamming books

▶ **Scripture instructs ...**

"'In your anger do not sin': Do not let the sun go down while you are still angry" (Ephesians 4:26).

▶ **The manipulator implies ...**

"If you don't meet my expectations, you don't deserve any dialogue with me, but I'll make my point in other ways."

4 Scornful Sneer

- The curl of the lip
- The roll of the eyes
- The raising of the eyebrows
- The squinting of the eyes

▶ **In contrast, Isaiah 57:4 says ...**

"Whom are you mocking? At whom do you sneer and stick out your tongue? Are you not a brood of rebels, the offspring of liars?"

▶ **The manipulator implies ...**

"If you don't do what I want you to do, you don't deserve my respect."

5 Spiteful Sounds

- Audible sighs
- Deep grunts
- Long groans
- Smacked lips

▶ **Scripture reveals …**

"All my longings lie open before you, O LORD; my sighing is not hidden from you" (Psalm 38:9).

▶ **The manipulator implies …**

"If you don't meet my expectations, I will let you know how perturbed I am with you."

6 Suppressed Support[17]

- Withholding compliments
- Withholding gifts
- Withholding affection
- Withdrawing presence

▶ **The apostle Paul said to the Corinthian church …**

"We are not withholding our affection from you, but you are withholding yours from us" (2 Corinthians 6:12).

▶ **The manipulator implies …**

"If you don't meet my standards, you will not get any attention whatsoever from me."

7 Strategic Stalling[18]

- Intentionally slow
- Intentionally late
- Intentionally not hearing
- Intentionally forgetful

▶ **In contrast, 1 Corinthians 13:5 says …**

"[Love] is not rude."

▶ **The manipulator implies …**

"If you don't give me control, I'll take control in other ways."

8 Sniveling Sobber[19]

- Timed tears
- Subtle sniffles
- Tearful stories
- Extended crying

▶ **In contrast, Hosea 7:14 says …**

"They do not cry out to me from their hearts but wail upon their beds. They gather together for grain and new wine but turn away from me."

▶ **The manipulator implies …**

"If you don't meet my emotional needs, I'll get your attention and make you feel guilty by falling apart."

Exit, "blessed" Jacob. Enter, "beaten to the punch" Esau.

He enters his father's presence with food in tow, eager for Isaac to begin eating and expecting the blessing to be bestowed. But Esau's world gets turned upside down with the following question from his father: *"Who are you?"*

"'I am your son,' he answered, 'your firstborn, Esau.'"

"Isaac trembled violently and said, 'Who was it, then, that hunted game and brought it to me? I ate it just before you came and I blessed him—and indeed he will be blessed!'" (Genesis 27:32–33).

Esau breaks out with a loud and bitter cry, having no trouble identifying his impersonator and devising a dastardly plan of his own.

Every ruse has repercussions whether the initiator is relative, friend, or foe, but especially serious repercussions when the ruse affects a person's relationship with God.

Although people may have a heart for the Lord, they may tend to be spiritually manipulative.

Motivating God's People

QUESTION: "If spiritual manipulation is not used, what will motivate people to follow God's will?"

ANSWER: No manipulation is needed to motivate people—instead God Himself is the motivator. The Bible says that the Lord writes His laws on our hearts and minds.

"This is the covenant I will make with them ... says the Lord. I will put my laws in their hearts, and I will write them on their minds" (Hebrews 10:16).

▶ He prompts you to do His will.

"It is God who works in you to will and to act according to his good purpose" (Philippians 2:13).

▶ He provides you with the power to do His will.

"The one who calls you is faithful and he will do it" (1 Thessalonians 5:24).

▶ He puts His words in your mind and reminds you to do His will.

"The Counselor, the Holy Spirit, whom the Father will send in my name, will teach you all things and will remind you of everything I have said to you" (John 14:26).

Ultimately, because Christ indwells every true Christian, we have both His will and His supernatural power to do His will.

"His divine power has given us everything we need for life and godliness." And the next verse tells us why—we *"participate in [Christ's] divine nature"* (2 Peter 1:3–4).

Spiritual Manipulation or Biblical Obedience

QUESTION: "What is the difference between spiritual manipulation and biblical obedience?"

ANSWER: Obedience is the act of conforming outwardly to God's righteous standard and inwardly to the character of Christ through the enabling grace of God.

▶ In *manipulation*, the resource is self-effort—the motive is self-promotion. Manipulation results in pride and is based on a performance-based approach to God.

▶ In *obedience*, the resource is the Spirit of God—the motive is to glorify God. Obedience results in humility and approaching God on the basis of Christ's performance.

"The grace of God that brings salvation has appeared to all men. It teaches us to say 'No' to ungodliness and worldly passions, and to live self controlled, upright and godly lives in this present age, while we wait for the blessed hope—the glorious appearing of our great God and Savior, Jesus Christ, who gave himself for us to redeem us from all wickedness and to purify for himself a people that are his very own, eager to do what is good" (Titus 2:11–14).

Before Esau turns his attention to the *"rightly named Jacob"* (Genesis 27:36), he pleads with Isaac.

"'Bless me—me too, my father! … Do you have only one blessing, my father? Bless me too, my father!' Then Esau wept aloud" (Genesis 27:34, 38).

But the subsequent words of Isaac for Esau are pitiful compared to what has been proclaimed for Jacob. *"Your dwelling will be away from the earth's richness, away from the dew of heaven above. You will live by the sword and you will serve your brother. But when you grow restless, you will throw his yoke from off your neck"* (Genesis 27:39–40).

The tragic turn of events leads Esau to look ahead to "payback time." *"The days of mourning for my father are near; then I will kill my brother Jacob"* (Genesis 27:41).

Rebekah becomes aware of the planned revenge and decides to manipulate and deceive her husband again. She concocts a story about how Jacob needs to be sent away to live with her brother Laban in order to "protect" him from marrying a Hittite woman because Esau's Hittite wives so grieve her.

"I'm disgusted with living because of these Hittite women. If Jacob takes a wife from among the women of this land, from Hittite women like these, my life will not be worth living" (Genesis 27:46).

As the manipulative account concludes, Rebekah never sees her beloved son Jacob again, though the two brothers eventually reconcile.

Spiritually manipulative leaders are generally ... [20]

▶ **Authoritarian**—Implying that God communicates with His people only through a hierarchy of power

▶ **Image Conscious**—Seeking to present themselves as an image of perfect righteousness

▶ **Suppressive of Criticism**—Maintaining that those who question anything about the organization are actually challenging God's authority

▶ **Perfectionistic**—Condemning failure of any type or magnitude

▶ **Unbalanced**—Flaunting their distinctiveness to validate their claim of having a "special" relationship with God

▶ **Coercive**—Using any tactic available to persuade followers to disregard their own logic and do what the leaders demand

▶ **Intimidating**—Threatening members routinely with punishment or excommunication in order to gain compliance

▶ **Terrorizing**—By blaming the ministry's problems on the sins of the members

▶ **Condemning**—Heaping condemnation on outsiders and anyone who leaves the congregation

▶ **Discriminatory**—Telling average members their needs are less important than the needs of leaders

▶ **Legalistic**—Expecting members to make extreme sacrifices of money, time, and energy for the sake of the organization

▶ **Isolating**—Encouraging members to minimize or discontinue contact with family, friends, and the outside world

Most spiritual leaders who use spiritual manipulation present God as judge—a stern taskmaster—a judgmental judge. These spiritual manipulators have a misplaced confidence in themselves that leads to frustration, failure, and self-condemnation. The attitude toward others is prideful exclusivity, which produces frustration, fear, and resentment in others.

The Bible tells us …

> **"Such men are false apostles, deceitful workmen, masquerading as apostles of Christ."**
> **(2 Corinthians 11:13)**

CAUSES OF BEING MANIPULATED

Where did this maze of manipulation begin, and how did it begin?

The guile began in the Garden of Eden.

God pronounced everything He had made to be *"very good,"* but in time things became *very bad*. His perfect creation will be marred by manipulation, darkened by deception (Genesis 1:31).

A creature *"more crafty than any of the wild animals the LORD God had made"* (Genesis 3:1) plays a part in tarnishing the crowning jewel of God's creation—man and woman—and the stain of sin will mark all who come after them.

Eve is the first to be manipulated. She becomes mesmerized with what stands in the middle of the garden.

Satan speaks through a serpent, one apparently standing upright. But its destiny is known for sure—doomed to forever slither.

Cunning and clever, surreal and altogether satanic, the serpent draws Eve into a conversation that challenges the commands of God. *"Did God really say, 'You must not eat from any tree in the garden'?"* (Genesis 3:1).

The serpent's first strike is to cast doubt ... to knock Eve off-kilter, to send her mind spinning as to what God had actually said. He attacked her confidence in God's command by altering and misquoting God's prohibition against eating the fruit to include all the trees in the garden.

The serpent's second strike is literally to lie about the consequences of eating the forbidden fruit from *"the tree of the knowledge of good and evil."* God had said, *"When you eat of it you will surely die"* (Genesis 2:17).

However, Satan says, *"You will not surely die"* (Genesis 3:4).

Eve is enticed in every way by the appeal of the fruit. It looks good, it will taste good, but more so, it will make her *"like God"* or so the serpent says (Genesis 3:5).

Eve picks it, tastes it, and passes it on to Adam.

> "Therefore ... sin entered the world through one man, and death through sin, and in this way death came to all men."
> (Romans 5:12)

Satan did a masterful job of manipulation, one that laid a solid foundation for sin and set the stage for continued manipulation to flow through families from generation ... to generation ... to generation.

Background of Manipulation

In childhood you ...

▶ Had an over-controlling parent: domineering, critical, angry, punitive, or manipulative

▶ Experienced some type of abuse: verbal, emotional, physical, sexual, or spiritual

▶ Grew up in an abusive home environment

▶ Had "no voice" at home to share honest facts and feelings; you never dealt with your true feelings

▶ Learned about manipulation by watching your parents—with children, more is caught than taught

▶ Grew up in a "blaming home" that used guilt to control others

▶ Accepted blame for everything in childhood, a mind-set that easily set you up to be manipulated in adulthood

▶ Blamed everyone else for all of your wrongs, setting yourself up to become a manipulator

▶ Thought your "normal" was normal—but it was not

▶ Wanted to please others, but your "pleasing" was never pleasing enough

First Corinthians 13:11 tells us, *"When I was a child, I talked like a child, I thought like a child, I reasoned like a child. When I became a man, I put childish ways behind me."*

Feeling "Different"

Because you ...

▶ Were born with a disability

▶ Were unsuccessful in school

▶ Were taunted by schoolmates

▶ Were humiliated by a teacher

▶ Were shamed by a coach

▶ Were taught that God was ready to punish every bad thought

▶ Were told you could never please God

First Samuel 16:7 tells us, *"The LORD does not look at the things man looks at. ... The LORD looks at the heart."*

There is no record that Adam wrestled with his conscience or even attempted to wrestle the forbidden fruit from Eve's hand.

The Bible says, *"She also gave some to her husband, who was with her, and he ate it"* (Genesis 3:6). Period. Case closed. End of story. Well—not quite.

The sweetness of the fruit quickly sours as *"the eyes of both of them were opened"* (Genesis 3:7), and they realize—for the first time—they are naked. A flood of emotions sweeps over them: discomfort with their nakedness, vulnerability, guilt, alienation, and fear.

The devil accomplished his goal. He succeeded in bringing sin into God's creation and into the lives of His cherished couple. He challenged God's power and control, and now he feels he has won the battle.

> **"You [Satan] said in your heart ...
> 'I will make myself like the Most High.'"**
> **(Isaiah 14:13–14)**

▶ Make them feel guilty

▶ Present reality the way they want others to see it

▶ Get others to believe what they want them to believe

▶ Control others to protect themselves, fearing being "taken advantage of"

▶ Get "their way"

▶ Maintain a dependent relationship even when the friendship is unhealthy

▶ Avoid having to meet their own obligations and responsibilities in life

▶ Appear positive when they actually feel negative toward someone

▶ Rescue them or clean up after their problems

▶ Make others feel sorry for them and take responsibility for them

▶ Intentionally confuse others with unclear messages

▶ Get others to do for them what they would not otherwise choose to do

▶ Get away with not having to meet their own obligations in life

▶ Keep them from moving away from the relationship

▶ Get others to feel responsible for them or for their welfare

▶ Control the emotions and reasoning of the ones being manipulated

▶ Win the battle for control

You clearly see in Scripture …

> **"The heart is deceitful above all things and beyond cure. Who can understand it?"**
> **(Jeremiah 17:9)**

WHY WOULD Someone Succumb to Manipulation?

After succumbing to manipulation, Adam and Eve sew fig leaves together for clothing—uneasy with their nakedness. They hear the Lord walking in the garden, and rather than respond to Him, they hide from Him.

"The LORD God called to the man, 'Where are you?'" (As if He has no clue!)

Then Adam answers, *"I heard you in the garden, and I was afraid because I was naked; so I hid."*

God replies, *"Who told you that you were naked? Have you eaten from the tree that I commanded you not to eat from?"* (Genesis 3:9–11).

The silver-tongued snake manipulates the first pair with a promise: The forbidden fruit will make them wise. Now, having succumbed to manipulation, the couple actually attempts to manipulate their Creator, proving that rather than becoming wise, they have become merely weak-minded.

Typically, the manipulated don't understand why they are so easily manipulated. They fail to realize that it is as simple as choosing to whom they will respond: their manipulator or their Maker.

Typically, they have a combination of the following:

▶ Misplaced Dependence on the Manipulator[22]

- "I must have you in my life."
- "I need you to give meaning and purpose to my life."
- "I have to have your approval in order to feel significant."

Solution

"Stop trusting in man, who has but a breath in his nostrils. Of what account is he?" (Isaiah 2:22).

▶ Misplaced Priorities[23]

- "What others think is more important than anything else."
- "The judgment and opinion of others takes precedence over my own."
- "The end justifies the means, even if it involves violating my conscience."

Solution

"I strive always to keep my conscience clear before God and man" (Acts 24:16).

▶ Fear of Disapproval

- "I can't say *no* for fear of making someone angry at me."
- "I'm afraid of being rejected."
- "I can't take a stand against someone whose approval I need."

Solution

"Do not fear the reproach of men or be terrified by their insults. For the moth will eat them up like a garment; the worm will devour them like wool. But my righteousness will last forever, my salvation through all generations" (Isaiah 51:7–8).

▶ Performance-based Acceptance

- "I am accepted only because of what I do."
- "I have value only if my work is acceptable."
- "I have worth only if I please others."

Solution

"The very hairs of your head are all numbered. Don't be afraid; you are worth more than many sparrows" (Luke 12:7).

▶ Defensiveness about the Relationship

- "I am not seeing objectively that the relationship is unhealthy."
- "I am not facing the need for a change in the relationship."

- "I am not willing to do anything about changing the relationship."

Solution

"Fear of man will prove to be a snare, but whoever trusts in the LORD is kept safe" (Proverbs 29:25).

▶ Loss of Independence

- "I am not allowed to make independent plans."
- "I am not permitted to have 'alone time.'"
- "I am not encouraged to spend money or time separately."

Solution

"My salvation and my honor depend on God; he is my mighty rock, my refuge" (Psalm 62:7).

▶ Loss of Confidence

- "I lose confidence when I am told the decision I made is wrong."
- "I feel uncomfortable when I am told my memory is wrong."
- "I feel stupid when I am told my perception is wrong."

Solution

"Encourage one another and build each other up, just as in fact you are doing" (1 Thessalonians 5:11).

▶ Loss of Identity (Controlled by the Manipulator's Personality or Power)

- "I am consumed by the actions of the manipulator."
- "I am consumed by what the manipulator wants and desires."
- "I am consumed by what the manipulator threatens to do."

Solution

"It is for freedom that Christ has set us free. Stand firm, then, and do not let yourselves be burdened again by a yoke of slavery" (Galatians 5:1).

▶ Loss of Objectivity (Makes Excuses for the Manipulator)

- "They don't mean to act that way."
- "They can't help being that way."
- "They aren't really bothering me."

Solution

"Better is open rebuke than hidden love" (Proverbs 27:5).

Misplaced Dependency

QUESTION: "How is my dependency misplaced if I am being manipulated?"

ANSWER: If you assume you must meet all the needs and fulfill all the expectations of someone else—then you are depending too much on yourself. You are taking the role God alone should have. Likewise, if you assume someone must meet all of your needs and fulfill all of your expectations—then you are depending too much on them. You are putting a person in the role God alone should have.

This is what the Lord says ...

"Cursed is the one who trusts in man, who depends on flesh for his strength and whose heart turns away from the LORD. ... But blessed is the man who trusts in the LORD, whose confidence is in him."
(Jeremiah 17:5, 7)

Call it a classic case of "passing the buck."

Adam admits eating the forbidden fruit, but not before he couches his confession in condemnation of Eve and even hints that God is at fault as well. He possibly even has an index finger pointing straight at Eve, but maybe not at God. Adam speaks the following words:

"The woman you put here with me—she gave me some fruit from the tree, and I ate it" (Genesis 3:12). *You* put her here, God. *She* gave me the fruit. *Then* I ate it.

Fortunately for Adam, God has patience with Adam and turns His gaze to Eve.

When God questions Eve, her index finger is likely stretched toward the serpent. *"The serpent deceived me, and I ate"* (Genesis 3:13).

Although the couple was not brainwashed, they did buy into Satan's deception hook, line, and sinker. Now, they are scrambling to justify themselves.

▶ **Verbal Brainwashing**

- **Intimidation**: Implying that your failure to comply with all demands, attitudes, or beliefs of the manipulator will result in severe consequences

- **Indoctrination**: Repeatedly implanting messages contrary to your presently held values

- **Discrediting**: Belittling your "outside" family and friends who disagree with the manipulator

- **Degrading**: Engaging in name-calling, insults, ridicule, and humiliation

- **Labeling**: Claiming that your thoughts are childish, stupid, or crazy

Psalm 35:20 tells us ...

"They do not speak peaceably, but devise false accusations against those who live quietly in the land."

▶ **Emotional Brainwashing**

- **Isolation**: Depriving you of all outside sources of emotional and social support

- **Excessive compliance**: Militantly enforcing trivial demands

- **Ignoring**: Withdrawing emotional support, but later denying that they had

- **Exploiting**: Using you or someone else close to you for self interests or gain

Psalm 10:2 tells us ...

"In his arrogance the wicked man hunts down the weak, who are caught in the schemes he devises."

An omniscient God is nobody's fool, and soon catastrophic consequences befall all three parties involved—consequences that are still being experienced by you and me today. Nature and the serpent are cursed; the cunning creature is forced to crawl on its belly forever. Painful toil was pronounced for Adam, and increased pain in childbirth for Eve, among other judgments. But God's most devastating declaration of all—death will become part of the human experience.

Satan's lie, "You can sin and get away with it," is crushed by the weight of God's truth—sin will be punished.

But even in the midst of divine judgment, divine love and provision are declared for sinful mankind. Genesis 3:15 contains the "proto-evangelium," the first "good news" recorded in Scripture, the prophesying of a victorious Savior. Here God addresses the serpent:

> **"I will put enmity between you
> and the woman, and between your offspring
> and hers; he will crush your head,
> and you will strike his heel."
> (Genesis 3:15)**

The couple had been manipulated and deceived. They believed a lie, but God knew the truth.

▶ WRONG BELIEF OF THE MANIPULATOR:

"This is a dog-eat-dog world, a survival of the fittest world. Therefore, I can't trust anyone to meet my needs. If I don't take control of the people and circumstances in my life, my needs for love, for significance, and for security will never be met."[24]

RIGHT BELIEF OF THE MANIPULATOR:

"God loves me sacrificially and has promised to meet my needs. Therefore, I will love others with His love rather than use others in an attempt to gain the love, significance, and security only God can give me."

"Love one another. As I have loved you, so you must love one another." (John 13:34)

▶ WRONG BELIEF OF THE ONE MANIPULATED:

"I must have the approval of others in order to feel good about myself."[25]

RIGHT BELIEF OF THE ONE MANIPULATED:

"I do not need the approval of others because God accepts me totally and loves me unconditionally, and He alone will meet all of my inner needs. [26]

"The LORD will guide you always; he will satisfy your needs in a sun-scorched land and will strengthen your frame. You will be like a well-watered garden, like a spring whose waters never fail." (Isaiah 58:11)

STEPS TO SOLUTION

What goes around comes around. And the sad saga of the manipulative patriarchs and their descendants continues.

After Jacob finagled Esau out of his birthright blessings, it is now Jacob's turn to get "had."

After fleeing to Haran to live with his uncle Laban, Jacob falls in love with Laban's beautiful daughter Rachel and strikes a deal with Laban. *"So Jacob served seven years to get Rachel, but they seemed like only a few days to him because of his love for her"* (Genesis 29:20).

Laban throws a feast and gives his daughter's hand to Jacob in marriage, but it isn't Rachel's hand. The deceiver is deceived—it obviously runs in the family—and Jacob lies with Rachel's older sister Leah.

"When morning came, there was Leah! So Jacob said to Laban, 'What is this you have done to me? I served you for Rachel, didn't I? Why have you deceived me?'" (Genesis 29:25).

"Why have you deceived me?" Jacob's father, Isaac, might have asked Jacob that very same question years before. Now the "trickster" himself has been tricked.

Laban explains it's not customary for a younger daughter to marry before the older. He instructs

Jacob to finish the week of wedding festivities with Leah and then he'll get Rachel *"in return for another seven years of work. And Jacob did so"* (Genesis 29:27–28).

The tangled mess of manipulation ensnares and traps all who seek to please either themselves or others rather than God.

Key Verses to Memorize

FOR THE ONE MANIPULATED:

"Am I now trying to win the approval of men, or of God? Or am I trying to please men? If I were still trying to please men, I would not be a servant of Christ" (Galatians 1:10).

FOR THE MANIPULATOR:

"His divine power has given us everything we need for life and godliness through our knowledge of him who called us by his own glory and goodness. Through these he has given us his very great and precious promises, so that through them you may participate in the divine nature and escape the corruption in the world caused by evil desires" (2 Peter 1:3–4).

Key Passage to Read

1 Thessalonians 2:3–8

▶ *"For the appeal we make does not spring from error or impure motives, nor are we trying to trick you."* (v. 3)

▶ *"On the contrary, we speak as men approved by God to be entrusted with the gospel. We are not trying to please men but God, who tests our hearts."* (v. 4)

▶ *"You know we never used flattery, nor did we put on a mask to cover up greed—God is our witness."* (v. 5)

▶ *"We were not looking for praise from men, not from you or anyone else."* (v. 6)

▶ *"As apostles of Christ we could have been a burden to you, but we were gentle."* (vv. 6–7)

▶ *"We loved you so much that we were delighted to share with you not only the gospel of God but our lives as well, because you had become so dear to us."* (v. 8)

The Biblical Model

▶ The Appeal: v. 3
  - Without error
  - Without impure motives
  - Without trying to trick anyone

▶ The Appealer: v. 4
  - Approved by God
  - Trustworthy
  - Trying to please God, not men

▶ The Method of Appeal: vv. 5–6
  - Never use flattery

- Don't put on a mask to cover up greed
- Don't look for praise from men

▶ **The Basis of the Appeal: vv. 6–8**

- Not burdensome, but gentle
- Based on love
- Includes personal sharing and involvement

HOW TO Turn Away from Manipulation by Trusting God

Rachel has much in common with her husband's grandmother Sarah.

Like Sarah, Rachel is *beautiful, barren, and bereft of an heir.*

Sarah attempted to solve her problem by offering her maidservant Hagar to Abraham in hopes of raising a family through her. The result was a son, but not the promised covenant son, Isaac. Rachel, wife of Sarah's grandson Jacob, is in the same desperate circumstances, compounded by the fact that her own sister Leah has borne Jacob not one, not two, but four sons.

"When Rachel saw that she was not bearing Jacob any children, she became jealous of her sister. So she said to Jacob, 'Give me children, or I'll die!'"
(Genesis 30:1)

As with Sarah, God was planning to bless Rachel with her husband's most blessed son of all (Joseph). But like Sarah, Rachel too offers her own maidservant (Bilhah), who gives Jacob two sons. And the manipulative cycle goes on from generation to generation to generation, down through the annals of Hebrew history.

The solution to manipulation is never more manipulation, but is rather moving away from manipulation and moving toward God.

What Is the First Step You Can Take?

The first step for you to take on the Lord's path away from manipulation is to enter into a loving relationship with Him. To help you understand the relationship that God wants to have with you, here are four points from His Word that you need to know.

#1 God's Purpose for You is *Salvation*.

What was God's motive in sending Christ to earth?

To express His love for you by saving you! The Bible says …

"God so loved the world that he gave his one and only Son, that whoever believes in him shall not perish but have eternal life. For God did not send his Son into the world to condemn the world, but to save the world through him" (John 3:16–17).

What was Jesus' purpose in coming to earth?

To forgive your sins, to empower you to have victory over sin, and to enable you to live a fulfilled life! Jesus said …

"I have come that they may have life, and have it to the full" (John 10:10).

#2 Your Problem is *Sin.*

What exactly is sin?

Sin is living independently of God's standard—knowing what is right, but choosing what is wrong. The Bible says …

"Anyone, then, who knows the good he ought to do and doesn't do it, sins" (James 4:17).

What is the major consequence of sin?

Spiritual "death"—eternal separation from God. Scripture reads …

"Your iniquities [sins] have separated you from your God. … For the wages of sin is death, but the gift of God is eternal life in Christ Jesus our Lord" (Isaiah 59:2; Romans 6:23).

#3 God's Provision for You is the *Savior.*

Can anything remove the penalty for sin?

Yes! Jesus died on the cross to personally pay the penalty for your sins.

"God demonstrates his own love for us in this: While we were still sinners, Christ died for us" (Romans 5:8).

What can keep you from being separated from God?

Belief in (entrusting your life to) Jesus Christ as the only way to God the Father. Jesus says …

"I am the way and the truth and the life. No one comes to the Father except through me" (John 14:6).

#4 Your Part is *Surrender.*

Give Christ control of your life—entrusting yourself to Him.

"Jesus said to his disciples, 'If anyone would come after me, he must deny himself and take up his cross [die to your own self-rule] and follow me. For whoever wants to save his life will lose it, but whoever loses his life for me will find it. What good will it be for a man if he gains the whole world, yet forfeits his soul?'" (Matthew 16:24–26).

Place your faith in (rely on) Jesus Christ as your personal Lord and Savior and reject your "good works" as a means of earning God's approval.

"It is by grace you have been saved, through faith—and this not from yourselves, it is the gift of God—not by works, so that no one can boast" (Ephesians 2:8–9).

The moment you choose to believe in Him— entrusting your life to Christ—He gives you His Spirit to live inside you. Then the Spirit of Christ gives you His power to live the fulfilled life God has planned for you. If you want to be fully forgiven by God and become the person God created you to be, you can tell Him in a simple, heartfelt prayer like this:

PRAYER OF SALVATION

"God, I want a real relationship with You.
I admit that many times I've chosen
to go my own way instead of Your way.
Please forgive me for my sins.
Jesus, thank You for dying on the cross
to pay the penalty for my sins.
Come into my life to be
my Lord and my Savior.
Change me from the inside out and make
me the person You created me to be.
In Your holy name I pray.
Amen."

What Can You Expect Now?

If you sincerely prayed this prayer, look at what God says!

"Trust in the LORD with all your heart
and lean not on your own understanding;
in all your ways acknowledge him,
and he will make your paths straight."
(Proverbs 3:5–6)

The Hebrew king, Ahab, wants Naboth's vineyard, and the queen is going to make sure he gets it.

King Ahab tries to negotiate with Naboth for his vineyard near the palace hoping to make it a vegetable garden. But it is a no go. *"The LORD forbid that I should give you the inheritance of my fathers,"* Naboth declared (1 Kings 21:3).

Angry and dejected, Ahab lies on his bed and sulks, refusing to eat. His wife, Jezebel, inquires about his sullen state and tells him to cheer up—she'll get that vineyard, no problem. She maneuvers people and manipulates a false scenario. *"Proclaim a day of fasting and seat Naboth in a prominent place among the people. But seat two scoundrels opposite him and have them testify that he has cursed both God and the king. Then take him out and stone him to death."* (1 Kings 21:9–10)

The queen's directive is obeyed—and Naboth is sacrificed for a vegetable garden. When Ahab goes to take possession of the property, he finds God's man for the times, Elijah the Tishbite. Elijah doesn't have much to say about vegetables, but he does have a thing or two to say about dogs—and divine punishment. Elijah declares what the Lord says: *"'In the place where dogs licked up Naboth's blood, dogs will lick up your blood—yes, yours!'*

*... And also concerning Jezebel the L*ORD *says: 'Dogs will devour Jezebel by the wall of Jezreel.'"* (1 Kings 21:19, 23)

While Ahab may have manipulated Jezebel to get the vegetable garden he wanted, there can be no doubt about Jezebel's manipulating the death of Naboth. Clearly, some manipulation is so subtle and covert it is difficult to recognize, both by the manipulator and the manipulated. However, objective observers may have no difficulty at all recognizing a spade as a spade, a shyster as a shyster. If you question whether you sometimes, or oftentimes, engage in manipulative maneuvers, honestly answer the following questions:

Have you ever been told ...

___ You are manipulative or controlling?

___ You are too possessive or confining?

___ You do not take responsibility?

___ You are always "nicer" to *others*?

___ You tend to overreact?

___ You have difficulty admitting when you are wrong?

___ You usually insist on getting your way?

___ You use anger or blame to motivate others?

___ You have difficulty putting problems "on the table" for logical discussions?

___ You have a destructive style of interaction?

Scripture makes it clear how people feel about crafty manipulators:

**"A quick-tempered man does foolish things,
and a crafty man is hated."
(Proverbs 14:17)**

HOW TO Say "No" to Manipulators

He has beguiled an entire nation, but Hananiah's deception proves to be his doom.

The nation of Judah is facing 70 years of captivity in Babylon as discipline for a multitude of sins that were being committed against the Lord. God's prophet, Jeremiah, wears a wooden yoke on his neck to symbolize subjection to Babylon's king, Nebuchadnezzar.

But Hananiah has a far more appealing message and manages to manipulate the nation with false prophecies. He foretells liberation from their captors within two years, with all exiles returning home and all articles from the temple safely restored. Additionally, Hananiah removes the yoke from Jeremiah's neck and breaks it to "represent" the end of Nebuchadnezzar's reign over Judah.

However, Hananiah's sway over Judah leads to a squaring-off with the Sovereign. *"The prophet Jeremiah said to Hananiah the prophet, 'Listen, Hananiah! The Lord has not sent you, yet you have persuaded this nation to trust in lies. Therefore, this is what the Lord says: "I am about to remove you from the face of the earth. This very year you are going to die, because you have preached rebellion against the Lord"'* (Jeremiah 28:15–16).

Rather than taking the path of least resistance by going along with Hananiah, Jeremiah said *no* to his lies and said *yes* to God's truth even when it wasn't popular to do so. Jeremiah obviously agreed with the admonition of Jesus that was given hundreds of years later.

"Let your 'Yes' be 'Yes,' and your 'No,' 'No.'"
(Matthew 5:37)

You too can say no to manipulators by … [27]

▶ **Not buying a certain product**

Affirm the item: "I feel sure your product is very good."

Then say *no*: "However, it does not fit within my budget, and I really don't have a need for it." (Repeat, if challenged.)

▶ **Not accepting a certain assignment**

Affirm the project: "I think what you are doing is great, and I'm glad you have been able to make the time to do it."

Then say *no*: "However, I am so committed in other endeavors that I cannot in good conscience undertake another. I feel sure the Lord will put this project on the heart of someone else so that the need will be met."

▶ **Not agreeing to meet a particular need of someone else**

Affirm the need: "I know a great need exists for teachers with the young people."

Then say *no*: "However, I also know I am not led by the Lord to do this. Therefore, God must have equipped and called someone else to meet this need, and I would not want to rob that person of the opportunity to fulfill God's will."

▶ **Not contributing to a certain charity/church/ministry**

Affirm the charity: "I'm sure the mission of (_____) is admirable."

Then say *no*: "However, God has already led me to support several other ministries. I feel sure you will find others who are not already as heavily committed, and it will bless them to give."

▶ **Not accepting a date**

Affirm the person: "Thank you for asking me out."

Then say *no*: "However, I need to say no. But I am honored that you would ask."

▶ **Not marrying a person because someone says, "God told me that you should."**

Affirm the person: "I'm highly complimented that you think God has told you we are to marry."

Then say *no*: "However, I'm sure if God were truly speaking to you, He would have told me also. It sounds as though God might be preparing your heart for marriage. Therefore, I will pray that you will know who the right person is when the time is right."

▶ Not continuing in a relationship

Affirm the person: "I want God's best for both of us."

Then say *no*: "However, it's become apparent we are not bringing out the best in each other. Therefore, I know our relationship should not continue."

▶ Not submitting in marriage to what violates your conscience

Affirm the person: "I love you and want to be the best person I can be to you."

Then say *no*: "However, I know God does not want me to do anything that would violate my conscience, even if it means displeasing you. I want you to always be able to trust me to do what is right. I cannot do what you want because I do not believe it is right for me in God's sight."

▶ Not lying for another person

Affirm the feelings: "I sincerely care about your feelings and want to help you in every way possible."

Then say *no*: "However, I have made a commitment to Christ to be a person of integrity. Therefore, I cannot lie and say you are not here, but I can say you are unavailable and then take a message."

"A truthful witness gives honest testimony, but a false witness tells lies."
(Proverbs 12:17)

As you prayerfully practice saying *no* to manipulators, practice saying *yes* to God by consistently clinging to the Lord's promise to meet your inner needs for ... [28]

▶ **Sacrificial Love**

"The LORD appeared to us in the past, saying: 'I have loved you with an everlasting love; I have drawn you with loving-kindness.'" (Jeremiah 31:3)

▶ **Significance**

"'I know the plans I have for you,' declares the LORD, 'plans to prosper you and not to harm you, plans to give you hope and a future.'" (Jeremiah 29:11)

▶ **Security**

"The LORD himself goes before you and will be with you; he will never leave you nor forsake you. Do not be afraid; do not be discouraged." (Deuteronomy 31:8)

Their words are sweet as molasses, rolling off their lips, but they should stick like glue on their tongues.

They praise Jesus for having qualities they do not have themselves, *"Teacher, we know you are a man of integrity. You aren't swayed by men, because you pay no attention to who they are; but you teach the way of God in accordance with the truth"* (Mark 12:14).

It is a cunning commendation. The men are ready to trap Jesus, *"to catch him in his words"* (Mark 12:13).

The Pharisees, the religious leaders of the Jews, and the Herodians (Jews who support Herod and Roman political authority) actually despise Jesus, resenting His favor with the people, resenting His call to repentance. They hope to trip Jesus up over the issue of taxes, but He is fully aware of their manipulation and hypocrisy. Their snare comes encased in a question.

> **"Is it right to pay taxes to Caesar or not?
> Should we pay or shouldn't we?"**
> **(Mark 12:14–15).**

Jesus asks them for a coin and then offers up a few questions of His own.

> **"Whose portrait is this?
> And whose inscription?"**

> "'Caesar's,' they replied."
> "Then Jesus said to them, 'Give to Caesar
> what is Caesar's and to God what is God's.'"
> (Mark 12:16–17)

The manipulators walk away marveling.

While some snares come cloaked in a question, there are many questions regarding manipulation that are authentic and deserve a legitimate answer.

Ending a Manipulating Relationship

QUESTION: "I know I'm being manipulated. Why don't I end the relationship?"[29]

ANSWER: Probably because you fear losing the real or perceived benefits you are receiving in the relationship. Ask yourself what it will cost you to walk away. Even unhealthy relationships can provide a sense of feeling loved, significant, and secure.[30] A desperate fear of rejection often paralyzes a person who is trying to make healthy decisions. The belief is often that "any relationship is better than no relationship." In such cases it is helpful to remember the words of King David and then to practice them:

> "I sought the LORD,
> and he answered me;
> he delivered me from all my fears."
> (Psalm 34:4)

Knowing When You Are Being Manipulated

QUESTION: "How do I know whether I am being manipulated?"

ANSWER: Evaluate: Am I doing this to gain someone's approval or because I fear losing someone's approval? Will my decision affect my relationship with the person who wants me to do this? Or am I doing this because it is the right thing for me to do? Is my motive to please a person or to please God?

"Am I now trying to win the approval of men, or of God? Or am I trying to please men? If I were still trying to please men, I would not be a servant of Christ." (Galatians 1:10)

People have been coerced into doing any number of things in the name of love, loyalty, and kindness. If Sarah had encouraged her husband to trust God, rather than submitting to his request to misrepresent their relationship, they might have been spared much sorrow and shame.

Submission and Manipulation

QUESTION: "Is a wife still being submissive to her husband when she takes a stand against his manipulation?"

ANSWER: No wife is to submit to a husband's sinful request. And manipulation is a sin because faith is placed not in the Lord but in the manipulative tactics used. Therefore, if a wife perpetuates the sinful pattern of her husband by engaging in sin with him, she is not helping him but is rather hindering him. She is both endorsing and encouraging his sinful behavior because … [31]

> **"Everything that does not**
> **come from faith is sin."**
> **(Romans 14:23)**

HOW TO Maneuver Out of Being Manipulated

Clearly, Jesus did not yield to the manipulative maneuvers of the religious leaders of His day. Every tactic and trick they tried on Him, Jesus thwarted. None of them worked. He never yielded to their pressure or fell for their ploys. He was never sidelined by their schemes or sidetracked by their scenarios. They never diverted His focus from His Father's will or His purpose.

> **"'My food,' said Jesus, 'is to do the will of**
> **him who sent me and to finish his work.**
> **… For I have come down from heaven**
> **not to do my will but to do the will**
> **of him who sent me.'"**
> **(John 4:34; 6:38)**

If it is your heart's desire to be like Jesus and no longer succumb to the shenanigans of selfish manipulators, apply the directives in the following acrostic on DEPENDENCY.

Decide not to be dependent on the manipulator.

- Decide you have had an unhealthy dependent relationship and confess it to God.

- Decide you want a healthy relationship that glorifies God.

- Decide you will be dependent on the Lord to meet your deepest needs.

"God will meet all your needs according to his glorious riches in Christ Jesus." (Philippians 4:19)

Expect exasperation from the manipulator.

- Don't expect the manipulator to understand or agree with your decisions.

- Don't expect the manipulator to acknowledge being manipulative.

- Don't expect the manipulator to be willing to stop controlling you and to set you free.

"Since you are my rock and my fortress, for the sake of your name lead and guide me. Free me from the trap that is set for me, for you are my refuge." (Psalm 31:3–4)

Prepare yourself for pain.

- Accept the fact that change is painful. However, in time peace will reign in your heart, and in time peace may also reign in your relationship.

- Accept the fact that change will be resisted by the manipulator.

- Accept the fact that if you don't change, you will stay in pain and peace will elude you.

"I have no peace, no quietness; I have no rest, but only turmoil." (Job 3:26)

Examine the methods of the manipulator.

- Ask God to open your eyes to the ways you have been manipulated.

- Ask yourself, "How am I being manipulated?" Then write out your tactics for change.

- Ask a trusted friend to help you see your blind spots and develop a plan of action.

"A prudent man sees danger and takes refuge, but the simple keep going and suffer for it" (Proverbs 22:3).

Notify the manipulator of the necessity for change.

- State that you have been wrong.

  "I've come to realize I've been wrong in the way I've related to you. At times I've not spoken up because I've been fearful. This is not healthy for either of us."

- State your commitment.

"I really do care about you. I want you to know that I am committed to change. I believe we can ultimately have a much healthier relationship."

Or, if it is not appropriate to continue in a relationship at all ...

- State your resolve.

"I cannot continue in a relationship with you and be the person I need to be before God."

"Since we are surrounded by such a great cloud of witnesses, let us throw off everything that hinders and the sin that so easily entangles, and let us run with perseverance the race marked out for us" (Hebrews 12:1).

Don't defend yourself.[32]

Although you will be accused of not being loving and caring ...

- You may choose to be silent, but don't use silence as a weapon.

- You may choose to state the truth once or repeat it several times. "I'm so sorry you feel that way. What you've said is not true—it does not reflect my heart."

- You may choose to say, "I understand that you think I am being heartless, but my intent is to become healthy."

"[There is] a time to tear and a time to mend, a time to be silent and a time to speak." (Ecclesiastes 3:7)

Expect experimentation with new strategies.[33]

- The manipulator may resort to using other methods to control you.

- The manipulator needs to know you are aware of these new methods.

- The manipulator needs to see that these new methods will not succeed.

"Wisdom will save you from the ways of wicked men, from men whose words are perverse." (Proverbs 2:12)

Nullify your need to meet all of the manipulator's needs.

- Realize that God didn't design anyone to meet ALL the needs of another person.

- Realize if you meet all of the manipulator's needs, then the manipulator won't recognize the need for the Lord.

- Realize you need to redirect the manipulator's focus to the Lord as the only true Need-Meeter.

"Delight yourself in the LORD and he will give you the desires of your heart. Commit your way to the LORD; trust in him and he will do this." (Psalm 37:4–5)

Commit Galatians 1:10 to memory.

- Recognize the truth in Galatians 1:10 by saying it at least three times a day.

    "Am I now trying to win the approval of men, or of God? Or am I trying to please men? If I

were still trying to please men, I would not be a servant of Christ." (Galatians 1:10)

- Realize that the only approval you need comes from God.

  "Am I now trying to win the approval of men, or of God? Or am I trying to please men?" (Galatians 1:10)

- Remember to live out this truth because you are Christ's servant.

  "Am I now trying to win the approval of men, or of God? Or am I trying to please men? If I were still trying to please men, I would not be a servant of Christ." (Galatians 1:10)

Yield to pleasing the Lord first.

- See that Jesus was not a "peace at any price" person. He said …

  "Do not suppose that I have come to bring peace to the earth. I did not come to bring peace, but a sword." (Matthew 10:34)

- See that if you want to be like Jesus, you too must not be a "peace at any price" person.

- See that you are to keep your trust in God and to fear no one.

  "In God I trust; I will not be afraid. What can man do to me?" (Psalm 56:11)

Paul gazes throughout the teeming metropolis and finds himself *"greatly distressed"* (Acts 17:16).

Athens is a city flourishing on philosophical exchange, and the free flow of ideas, but it is a city *"full of idols"* (Acts 17:16). Everywhere are statues of gold, silver, and stone, images made by man's design and skill. Paul preaches about an *invisible* God, one so powerful He can never be contained in an inanimate object. How will the Athenians handle *that* idea?

Because many people in Athens spend their time *"doing nothing but talking about and listening to the latest ideas"* (Acts 17:21), they undoubtedly are easy targets for manipulation and deception. But Paul's heart is to *persuade* the lost about the living Christ. As he *reasons* (Acts 17:17) in the marketplace day after day, he gains the attention of a group of philosophers.

Up to this point, Paul has resisted any temptation to be manipulative, but now he must engage with philosophically-minded unbelievers while avoiding manipulative conversation.

If you find yourself in a similar situation with a stranger or with someone you know quite well, walk through the following steps:

After Determining Your Plan of Action ...

1 State clearly what you are willing to accept and not willing to accept from the manipulator.

▶ Communicate your position in a positive way.

▶ Do not justify yourself. Do not be apologetic.

▶ "I want our relationship to continue, but ...
- "I am not willing to be controlled."
- "I am not willing to hear your accusations concerning (*name*) any longer."
- "I am not willing to endure the silent treatment from you."

▶ Keep what you say short and succinct.

Take to heart what the Bible says:

"A man of knowledge uses words with restraint, and a man of understanding is even-tempered." (Proverbs 17:27)

2 Announce the consequence you will enforce if the manipulator violates your requests.

▶ Your response should serve to disengage you from the manipulator.

▶ You cannot change the manipulator's behavior, but you can remove yourself from frequent exposure to unacceptable behavior.

▶ "I want to visit with you, but ...

- "If you call me a name again, I will leave for a period of time."
- "If you persist in making that accusation, I will terminate our conversation."
- "If you give me the silent treatment, I will find someone else to talk with."

▶ Consequences are part of God's divine plan that what we sow, we will reap.

Take to heart what the Bible says:

"A man reaps what he sows." (Galatians 6:7)

3 Enforce the consequence *every single time* the manipulative behavior occurs.

▶ Do not bluff! The manipulator needs to know you are going to consistently act on your words.

▶ In your mind and heart ...

- Say *no* to manipulation.
- Say *no* to pressure.
- Say *no* to control.

▶ Eventually, your manipulator will stop a manipulative tactic, but only after that tactic proves to be ineffective.

Take to heart what the Bible says:

"Let your 'Yes' be yes, and your 'No,' no." (James 5:12)

4 Absolutely do not negotiate.

▶ Since verbal manipulators do not use words fairly, negotiation will not work.

▶ Instead of "talking out" the problem, your manipulator will seek to wear you down.

▶ Simply state that you look forward to a renewed relationship when the behavior stops.

- "I am not willing to discuss this topic any longer."

- "I have stated clearly what I will not accept."

- "When you are ready to respect my requests, let me know. I look forward to enjoying being together at that time."

▶ Keep your words brief and to the point.

Take to heart what the Bible says:

"When words are many, sin is not absent, but he who holds his tongue is wise." (Proverbs 10:19)

5 Never "react" when your boundary is violated—only respond.

▶ Expect your boundary to be violated.

▶ Expect your boundary to be violated again and again!

▶ If you react, you will find yourself back under the control of the manipulator.

- Do not *cry* when feeling hurt.

- Do not *beg* when feeling fearful.

- Do not *explode* when feeling frustration.

▶ Respond by detaching yourself from the manipulator and enforcing your repercussions.

Take to heart what the Bible says:

"The end of a matter is better than its beginning, and patience is better than pride. Do not be quickly provoked in your spirit, for anger resides in the lap of fools." (Ecclesiastes 7:8–9)

6 Solicit the support of one or two wise, objective people to help you through this process.

▶ Include supporters as you analyze and identify the problem.

▶ Include supporters as you determine how to articulate your plan.

▶ Include supporters as you enforce the repercussions.

- Discuss the situation with your supporters.

- Discuss the tactics used on you.

- Discuss the plan of action.

▶ Include supporters—friend, mentor, counselor—to help you through this critical period.

Take to heart what the Bible says:

"Listen to advice and accept instruction, and in the end you will be wise." (Proverbs 19:20)

The time it takes to disassemble and disable a manipulative relationship is actually limited. But during that limited time, expect manipulative maneuvers and emotional ups and downs. Assume your actions will make the manipulator angry. Allow the person to react without your reacting. Do not seek to placate this person—it won't work. Think of this time period as comparable to having surgery. It is a painful experience, but it provides the only hope for healing if you are to have a new, healthy relationship.

Take to heart what the Bible says:

> **"Reckless words pierce like a sword,**
> **but the tongue of the wise brings healing."**
> **(Proverbs 12:18)**

And so they inquire …

"May we know what this new teaching is that you are presenting? You are bringing some strange ideas to our ears, and we want to know what they mean." (Acts 17:19–20)

What are the "strange ideas" Paul is preaching? The truths of the gospel, the death and resurrection of Jesus Christ. The Athenians have never heard of a "god" doing such a thing—"dying" and then coming back to life. Paul is brought before the Areopagus, the council that governs religious and educational matters, and begins his message by quoting an inscription. Then he said, *"As I walked around and looked carefully at your objects of worship, I even found an altar with this inscription:* TO AN UNKNOWN GOD. *Now what you worship as something unknown I am going to proclaim to you."* (Acts 17:23)

Paul presents God as the all-powerful, self-sufficient Creator, who governs the affairs of the world, gives all life its breath, calls people to repentance, and will one day judge the world through the One He has appointed—Jesus Christ. And Paul convincingly concludes that the true God is not some dreamed-up deity, a lofty image birthed in the recesses of man's imagination. *"He has given proof of this to all men by raising him from the dead"* (Acts 17:31).

As Paul so powerfully points out, the God of the Bible, the God who created everything is your Lord, your master, ruler, owner. Therefore, you are to …

▶ **Submit yourself to God's authority.** You are accountable to God first and human authorities second.

As God's Word says, *"We must obey God rather than men!"*(Acts 5:29)

▶ **Talk about your concerns with spiritual leaders who are not involved in your manipulative situation.** God desires peace, unity, and reconciliation between Christians.

As God's Word says, *"[We are to] be completely humble and gentle; be patient, bearing with one another in love. Make every effort to keep the unity of the Spirit through the bond of peace."* (Ephesians 4:2–3)

▶ **Consider how the spiritually manipulative attitude of others is impacting your spiritual life**, your relationships with family members and friends, and your sense of personal value.

As God's Word says, *"As iron sharpens iron, so one man sharpens another."* (Proverbs 27:17)

▶ **Separate yourself from manipulative situations** and seek out people who are encouraging.

As God's Word says, *"Encourage one another daily ... so that none of you may be hardened by sin's deceitfulness."* (Hebrews 3:13)

At times, the most spiritual sacrifice you can make is to stop being a people-pleaser. This means you must choose not to please another person so that you can please the Lord.

> To stop being manipulated, you must sometimes say *no* to people so you can then say *yes* to God.
>
> —June Hunt

SCRIPTURES TO MEMORIZE

What does God say about letting a person be too important? Is that like putting **other gods before** Him?

God says …

> *"You shall have no **other gods before** me."* (Exodus 20:3)

What will happen if I continue to live in **fear of man**?

> *"**Fear of man** will prove to be a snare, but whoever trusts in the LORD is kept safe."* (Proverbs 29:25)

What will happen if I try to **win the approval** of everyone and try to **please** them?

> *"Am I now trying to **win the approval** of men, or of God? Or am I trying to **please** men? If I were still trying to please men, I would not be a servant of Christ."* (Galatians 1:10)

What should I **not do** when I'm around a **hot-tempered** person?

> *"**Do not** make friends with a **hot-tempered** man, do not associate with one easily angered."* (Proverbs 22:24)

How does God view the person **who trusts in the Lord** and puts **confidence in Him**?

> *"Blessed is the man **who trusts in the LORD**, whose **confidence** is **in him**."* (Jeremiah 17:7)

Why should I **test** my **own actions** instead of **comparing** myself **to somebody else**?

> *"Each one should **test** his **own actions**. Then he can take pride in himself, without **comparing** himself **to somebody else**."* (Galatians 6:4)

How does the Bible contrast **a deceitful tongue** with one that **brings healing**?

> *"The tongue that **brings healing** is a tree of life, but **a deceitful tongue** crushes the spirit."* (Proverbs 15:4)

What is the difference between giving in to someone out of **love** and giving in **out of fear**?

> *"There is no **fear in love**. But perfect **love** drives **out fear**, because **fear** has to do with punishment. The one who fears is not made perfect in love."* (1 John 4:18)

Why should I **guard** my **heart**?

> *"Above all else, **guard** your **heart**, for it is the wellspring of life."* (Proverbs 4:23)

How can I have the **power** and **self-discipline** to stand up to a manipulator?

> *"God did not give us a spirit of timidity, but a spirit of **power**, of love and of **self-discipline**."* (2 Timothy 1:7)

NOTES

1. Lori Thorkelson Rentzel, *Emotional Dependency* (Downers Grove, IL: InterVarsity, 1990), 14; *Merriam Webster Online Dictionary*, s.v. "Manipulate," http://www.m-w.com.

2. *American Heritage Electronic Dictionary*, 4th edition (Boston: Houghton Mifflin, 2000), s.v. "Persuade." http://www.bartleby.com/61/17/P0211700.html.

3. Francis Brown, Samuel Rolles Driver, Charles Augustus Briggs, *Enhanced Brown-Driver-Briggs Hebrew and English Lexicon*, electronic ed. (Oak Harbor, WA: Logos Research Systems, 2000), s.v. "Jacob."

4. Tim Kimmel, *Powerful Personalities* (Colorado Springs: Focus on the Family, 1993), 29–42.

5. Kimmel, *Powerful Personalities*, 64–66.

6. Evertt L. Shostrom and Dan Montgomery, *The Manipulators* (Nashville: Abingdon, 1990), 12.

7. Kimmel, *Powerful Personalities*, 29–67. Kimmel divides the different manipulation techniques into three categories: (1) Aggressive, (2) Passive, and (3) Passive/Aggressive.

8. Kimmel, *Powerful Personalities*, 29–33.

9. Kimmel, *Powerful Personalities*, 36–39.

10. Kimmel, *Powerful Personalities*, 36–39; Jan Silvious, *Please Don't Say You Need Me: Biblical Answers for Codependency* (Grand Rapids: Pyranee Books, 1989), 56.

11. Kimmel, *Powerful Personalities*, 143–144; Barbara Sullivan, *The Control Grip: a Woman's Guide to Freedom from the Need to Manage People and Circumstances* (Minneapolis, MN: Bethany House, 1991), 67–69.

12. Kimmel, *Powerful Personalities*, 97.

13. Kimmel, *Powerful Personalities*, 61–62, 64–66.

14. Kimmel, *Powerful Personalities*, 64–66; Sullivan, *Control Grip*, 64–68.

15. Kimmel, *Powerful Personalities*, 29–67.

16. Kimmel, *Powerful Personalities,* 53–54.

17. Kimmel, *Powerful Personalities,* 46–48.

18. Kimmel, *Powerful Personalities,* 50–51.

19. Sullivan, *Control Grip,* 67–68; See Kimmel, *Powerful Personalities,* 61–62; Paul F. Schmidt, *Coping With Difficult People,* Christian Care Books, ed. Wayne E. Oates, vol. 6 (Philadelphia: Westminster, 1980), 100–101.

20. Edward Camella, "Religious Abuse," *The Remuda Review,* spring 2005, vol. 4, issue 2, p. 17–23.

21. James S. Messina, "Eliminating Manipulation," *LIVESTRONG.com,* http://www.livestrong.com/article/14680-eliminating-manipulation/.

22. Silvious, *Please Don't Say You Need Me,* 31; Kimmel, *Powerful Personalities,* 202.

23. Henry Cloud and John Townsend, *Boundaries: When to Say Yes, When to Say No, To Take Control of Your Life* (Grand Rapids: Zondervan, 1992), 199–201.

24. Lawrence J. Crabb, Jr., *Understanding People: Deep Longings for Relationship,* Ministry Resources Library (Grand Rapids: Zondervan, 1987), 15–16; Robert S. McGee, *The Search for Significance,* rev. and expanded ed. (Nashville: Word, 1998), 27–29.

25. Crabb, *Understanding People,* 15–16; McGee, *The Search for Significance,* 27–30.

26. McGee, *Search for Significance,* 65–67, 73.

27. Jo Coudert, "Nice Ways to Say No," *Reader's Digest,* January 1993, 135–137.

28. Crabb, *Understanding People,* 15–16; McGee, *The Search for Significance,* 27–30.

29. Shostrom and Montgomery, *The Manipulators,* 45–46.

30. Crabb, *Understanding People,* 15–16; McGee, *The Search for Significance,* 27–30.

31. Sullivan, *Control Grip,* 15.

32. Cloud and Townsend, *Boundaries,* 245.

33. Cloud and Townsend, *Boundaries,* 239–252.

June Hunt's HOPE FOR THE HEART minibooks are biblically-based, and full of practical advice that is relevant, spiritually-fulfilling and wholesome.

HOPE FOR THE HEART TITLES

www.aspirepress.com